Inspired Utterances

♥

♥

Diana

Silvia

Nicolaci

♥

Diana Silvia Nicolaci

Inspired Utterances
How Wonderful

The information contained in this book was gained through
personal experience, and through the practice of meditation.

ISBN: 978-0-646-58560-4

♥

♥

Contents

♥

My favourites

But of course I love it all

♥

♥

I feel as though the writer within me has connected, is that so?

What outstanding things can I write to prove that is so?

What marvellous trivia can we concoct?

What would you like to read my lovely my friend and companion within and without?

What shall we write together?

Let us begin.

♥

♥
Words

Words are my companion in times of distress.
Words are a gift beyond measure.
Words can astound and lift the spirit.
Words are a part of who I am.
Words will flow in times of need,
even in times of great confusion, my words
are given.

There are times of unknowing,
yet words can comfort, surprisingly,
they can comfort and lift up the spirit
because words are a connection.
They connect thought with spirit,
they connect one with the other,
they connect man with woman,
woman with child,
friend with foe.

♥

Words when given at the appropriate time
are a treasure beyond amounting.
Words are a gift, just one more of the many
gifts of life.
How thankful all must be to have so many
gifts.
Do my words end here?

Just wait and see............

♥

This book has come to you from God, from the Almighty God within me. There is a yearning in my soul to write something so profound, so touching, meaningful, helpful and inspiring so as to create rapture.

There is a lot of content in this book, at first I thought I would just publish the verses that came to me through meditation, but then I decided that it would be nicer for you to understand the motivation that brought me to the contents.

The words were written over many years and so therefore much of the content changes, as my own mind, life and spirit changes.

I am the vessel which my soul has used to express itself and the following is part of my journey.

I am no one special. I am just me, I like to write and I hope that through my writing we can share some kind of connection. I have my struggles as you will see more and more of throughout the pages. I hope that you will be

♥

touched by my words, and that you don't judge my craziness as we are all a little crazy.

There are three kinds of writing in this book perhaps you could call them the three parts of me.

♥

Meditation

Contemplation

Explanation

♥

♥

Divine Answers

Through Meditation

♥

I asked God, would God really save some people and not others and why? God replied.

♥
Beauty

Beauty is a presence a state of mind.
Beauty surrounds us all. It is the state of
mind which discerns it.

I have said two can be standing together on
the last day but I will gather up the one.
Two will be standing in the field and I will
take the one.

It is not that I will protect the one or choose
one above another.
It is that one has discerned me.
One and not the other has found me, only
through the perception can one find me.

One who is present.
Who can hear the birds chirping and who can
feel the sun upon the skin and who can smell

♥

the sweet smelling dew and who can taste the fruit of their labour and who can see the beauty around them.

They are the ones who will be saved, because they have saved themselves from the pain of not knowing.

♥
The Love Principle

There is a force which activates the mind.
This is the god force or the principle force.
There are many forces, the god force is the
principle force. I am God and the god force,
the Holy Spirit force actuating the mind.

I am the one who remembers all things and
the Holy Spirit brings back to you the
remembrance of me, of us, the complete. The
Holy Spirit is your force which you activate
at your request or your leisure. When you
feel comfortable enough to activate it.

Feel the comfort in me because we can be
comfortable. It is the remembering of what
was once one. The two will become one is the
remembrance. All will become one. All flesh
is flesh and all spirit is spirit, yet they are all

♥

one, the one principle, all else is a fantasy a lovely fantasy.

I am within, you can call on me at any time. This is the way out, to go within. To go within is the way out. Not without. You will not be without. You have all you need, nothing is without and no one will be without. You cannot find me. I am never without, because I am all and have all, I am never without. All will be revealed to all who seek. I am God, the God of eternity.

The love principle.

♥

♥

Is Satan Real?

♥
The River of Life

I am the river of life. Once united in love, in
union the river will run continually. I am the
way, I am the tree of life, the knowledge of
good and bad. I have all wisdom and all
understanding. I am the all and the
everything, there is no other.

Satan is a lie and the father of the lie. All will
know this, there is no such name, person,
place, thing. Satan is your own fear, your
own insecurity, your own anxiety, you have
made up the lie for your own sake, because
you don't want to be in union with me just as
we are in union always in everything.

What is darkness but alienation, you are an
alien in your own residence, in your own
household, you are un-united within your

♥

very being – unite – let us be one in our self.
The one is from within and where will it go?

Do not be afraid because I am the great and
almighty river of life. You are not just your
body, you are not just your spirit, you are not
just your mind, you are a reflection of light, a
ray of sunshine, a passing of the wind. You
are my creation.

Feel the joy when you fall away from the
darkness, feel the joy when you turn from the
lie and look directly at truth. This is an angel
of light when you come from nothing and find
you have everything, you are everything, feel
the wonder and excitement.

Satan is a lovely tool of creation, an actual
joy. Joy comes from the depths of despair,
from the murky depths the light shines

♥

through. When you can feel that everything separate from me is a lie, then you will find great joy.

I am who I am there is no other.

♥

Why do we have illness?

♥

Return To Me

Are you afraid of failure, of other people's opinion of you? You still have this to overcome because you are still thinking in separation that it is you alone who must conquer. You still don't believe or understand fully that we are one and that all things are already in perfection. You are healed and you are well but you think you are you and you don't feel the true connection of one.

I will reveal more to you as you yourself can handle because it is more sometimes than you can bear and I will not give you more than you can bear or you will feel that you are really going insane as many people will believe you are.

I am all, that is hard to conceive with your

♥

limited view on things. You can remain an individual as you wish, as you so choose. You can delight in your individuality but remember we are undivided, there is no division in me. You have been given free will. I have given the part of myself which you call you, free will. You can unite with me as you so choose.

Illness, there is no such thing. Hard to believe? Do you think you are going crazy now? There is no such thing, you have made it all up for your own reasons. You can now choose to give up the joke, give up the lie. Can you do this? Can you give up the lie of separation? When will you be ready? I am always here to return to.

When will you understand? You can return to me in an instant just as you are now, now,

♥

now, understand, in the twinkling of an eye.

You will know when you will know, until then make your life complete, be completely at ease with who you are and what you represent.

♥

What is Gods name and who is the true God?

♥

I Am

You wish to write of Gods name?

What is Gods Name?

Gods name is an alliance.

What is it you need to know?

Know and understand the meaning of Gods
name.

God is a God of all and therefore has many
names.

A name must stand up in a court of law.

Legally you are mine.

I own all and therefore you are my name.

What do you stand for?

My name is freedom. My name is abundance.

My name is pureness to the core.

♥

*People have called me many names and look
at the division it has caused.
My name is of no relevance,
I am all to all.*

*I am understanding, I am wisdom, I am
intelligence.
I am the light in a stormy place.
Whatever it is that you require of me then
that is my name,
that is who I am.
Whatever you need and whenever you need it
just call my name.*

*You do not need to know a specific name,
know that I am
just that
I am.*

♥

♥

I wrote the following verse after meeting a lady whose son had just died, he was her only child, she told me he was in his thirties and had died of an aneurysm. I could sense that her pain was so great that her own life no longer mattered to her. I felt her pain very deeply.

I went home and asked God to give me comforting words to share with people who suffer with the loss of a loved one. I myself had suffered greatly when my sister died and I know that this pain can be unbearable to humankind.

After my mediation I wrote freely without thinking, I didn't feel I was making any sense until I stopped to re read what I had written. I felt so much joy that I couldn't contain my tears, I had to walk away for a moment and then returned to finish it.

♥
Comforting Words

You ask for words, hauntingly beautiful words, spine chilling comforting words, but my spirit is beyond words and my love beyond boundaries. The body is bound but the spirit is unlimited. When you are in the body you are bound to the body. The spirit leaps with joy when it is released from the body.

My love is never ending, my love is there always in every way, death does not end my love and my love is boundless, unending. My love is pure with no restrictions, my love is not restricted to the body of a human, but when it is finished with the body it says goodbye, but not in pain and not in sorrow, but with love and thanks giving to the body it once possessed.

♥

There is no pain in love, there is no sorrow in love, there is no regret in love, there is just love. You will one day come to know of this love of which I am.

My love is not earth bound, bound to the earth or bound to a body, but is freely expressing itself at every moment. I am not sad at death. If you choose sadness, then so be it, be sad, but I know there is no sadness in death but only rejoicing. Sadness is from the earth below, love is from the realms above. You will one day find this comfort.

Words are only words, songs are only songs, poems are only poems, body is only body, spirit is only spirit.

You will know who I am when you will know and not before. Find comfort in just knowing

♥

that I am love, there
is nothing else, nothing more to add,
except this sacred truth,

Love Is All There Is.

Continued…

♥

I tell you this, you ask, will I see my loved one
again?, and I tell you, you will one
day come to know that one, because you will
come to know that loved one is you, you are
everyone and everyone is you. All the pieces
will one day come together and we will be
united once more in love.

These are not the words of madness but of
true wisdom, of ultimate truth, of ultimate
knowing. All will one day come to know of
this pure love.

When you hate someone, you are hating a
part of yourself. When you have affection for
someone you have affection for that part of
yourself. One day all will understand this
sacred truth.

♥

Everything is amazing fruit trees and sun

I am an amazing instrument, I am the sun
and the moon.
I am the rain and the snow, I am the full
moon in circle.
I am the tides of the ocean, I am the master
collector.
I am the master the key.

Where is your heart? Where is the heart of
happiness?
Where is the heart of joy?
Open to the master of the heart,
become open to all you ever dreamed of,
become open to your heart.

♥

*I can and will fill your heart with much joy
and much to enjoy.
The heart must first become open to this joy,
it must thirst for joy,
it must long for it.
The heart is the key to finding joy.*

*My love is in the song of the heart,
the song of the heart is what will sing to you,
and that is what you will follow.*

♥

Remember Me

I am the judge, I am the leader and the
conqueror.
I am the within and without of it all,
the ins and outs.
I am the fruit and the fruitage.

Behold a new day dawns,
the sun is rising.
Taste the new day, be intoxicated with what
it brings.
Delight in the moment.

Conquer, Overcome, Smile and bring good
cheer a new day awaits you,
joy is what it will bring,
laughter and happiness is what I promise you.

♥

*Do not wait you will not have to,
it is here now, there is no waiting, no longing
no hoping.*

*The kingdom of my love is in the new day,
the dawn of a new day and as the sun rises so
does my love and unwavering pledge to be
with you always in every breath you take
I am there with you my love.*

*I have said to you remember me
remember me remember me remember me
remember me remember me remember me
remember me.*

♥

I am me

Love does not seek to control.
If you love somebody,
if you love someone, set them free.
The truth will set you free.
Free to be who I am, to be the wonderful
creation of God.
To be unique and yet to be united.
To be a radiant shining light.
A light of love.
To be inspired, I feel the inspiration of god.
I am free to think as it pleases me, my
wonderful thoughts that I can think all day
long.
Happy to be in gods love and safety net that
covers me with peace of mind.
I am who I am. I am Gods child, Gods
daughter, Gods son. I am a part of the essence
of God.

♥

I am the likeness the droplet. I am the missing piece of the puzzle. I know who I am. I am me.

♥

Ever increasing love

I have been filled with holy spirit, the spirit of god is within me. I am filled with love, a transcendent love, which travels beyond all boundaries.

Love is the calling, it is due.

The time has come to you for your calling of love.

Beyond time is your love, ever increasing love beyond boundaries is your love, ever increasing love.

What is the calling my dear friend, what is your calling, do you understand?

We are all working towards the one calling

♥

which is to gain boundless love and unity.

Do not give up hope, for my love is real.
The only true reality is my love.

What is the calling my friend, what is now
due?

Be boundless yourself.

Be bountiful, leap with joy my love because
my love is real and coming to you quickly.

I will fill you up with love and thanksgiving
with glad tidings and sweeping joy.

Leap with joy, be buoyant with springing
steps of hope.

♥

Walk an air with love holding you up on high.

My spirit has filled you up with love increasing.

♥

♥

Birds Keep Calling

I feel that there is something in the language
of the birds.

The birds keep calling bringing a new
message.

The link to the outer world,
there brings new meaning a new light.
The outer world keeps calling
bringing you to a new world
the inner world.

There is meaning in the light
there is light
there is hope.

♥

Don't cry my love
don't cry for me.
I am going my way towards a new journey.
This journey has ended my love and a new
one awaits me.

Do not cry for me my love
as our journey is of one.
I have always delighted in you and I will
bring you back to me.

Remember the birds are calling
remember their song
it is, "I love you".

♥

I am a writer. I came here to write.
I am a writer.
Right now I am here
Writing.

☺

♥

♥

The Magic Of My Day

The following chapters are some little stories that have meaning or could I say morals or even lessons?

♥

New Towels

I set in my mind that I would like to buy some new towels, because I felt it was time to move forward and I wanted to freshen up my home and my life.

Driving along I was hoping that I would get the car park that I usually got, (being close to Christmas a car park is very hard to come by). I had faith that the car park I *normally* get would be there for me.

I drove around to where my usual car park was when I noticed it had been taken. A slight doubt crept into my mind, when all of a sudden a lady walked by and gestured for me to follow her because she was leaving, but then I noticed out of the corner of my eye a woman who was in *my* car park jump into her car to leave.

I ignored the kind lady who made the gesture, and took the park that I had planned to take.

After parking I noticed there was a commotion at the spot

♥

where I had been gestured to park. A young girl with her boyfriend had their indicator on to take the spot, when a man drove straight in without showing any concern for them. The young couple yelled out abuse and the older man yelled back, "you were going the wrong way".

As I walked along, a girl who had also witnessed the commotion said to me "Merry Christmas" joking about the spirit of Christmas in the others that were arguing. "I think they are both wrong", I said. We kept walking and I wished her a good day.

As I walked along I thought to myself, why had I seen this? When it occurred to me that if had followed the kind lady who had made the gesture, the whole argument would not have happened.

I would have taken the spot, the older man would have taken *my* spot and the young couple wouldn't have had any reason to argue because they were in fact going the wrong way and they weren't the kind of people to take someone else's spot.

♥

The lesson is to follow the right leads, not the ones you expect but the ones that are given as a gift. I realised I was too set in my ways and that if I was more flexible and thankful to the kind lady who gestured, this whole scenario wouldn't have happened.

I proceeded to walk into the store to buy the towels. I noticed some beautiful coloured ones which I loved straight away and thought how fresh they looked. Doubt crept in and I wondered, " would they fit my decor? Can I afford them"? I walked past them when I heard two ladies say how beautiful the towels were. I turned around and bought them and they were beautiful and fresh looking and suited my decor beautifully.

♥

♥

A Purposeful Accident ?

I have another magical day to share with you. In fact it is many days that all rolled into one and then kept going.

I'm sure you will find this story very interesting.

As I'm writing this, the day started 89 days ago, my son was hit by a car, in a purposeful accident.

My son worked on the same construction site as his father and they would travel to and from work together. The day before he was hit by the car, he didn't go to work because he had been out drinking all night with one of his friends, and was hung over.

When my husband woke to get ready for work that morning he noticed that our son wasn't home, being angry he phoned him on his mobile, no answer, so he phoned our sons friend, whom he assumed he would be with, his friend answered and then handed the phone to our son, when hearing his fathers voice, he hung up and turned the phone

♥

off.

My husband was furious and said, "when I see him I'm going to break both of his legs". He went to work and during the day told many a work mate that he was going to break both of his legs.

That afternoon when our son came home, my husband and I were not at all happy with him, there was tension in the air and we ignored him. He changed his clothes and went out again.

That night I felt a sick and nervous feeling in my whole body, as I tried to sleep I told my husband that I felt something bad was going to happen, he told me not to worry and to try to go to sleep.

At 1.30 in the morning my eldest daughter received a hysterical phone call saying that her brother had been hit by a car outside a pub. She came running into our bedroom to wake us up and tell us the terrible news. My immediate reaction was to prepare for the worst, my son may be dead

♥

or worse, paralysed, brain damaged who knows?

We quickly went to the scene and as we stopped the car I noticed hysterical young people all around crying, I thought' "oh my god this is bad". As the police tried to hold me back, I felt as though I was in one of those TAC adds where everything seemed to be staged and in slow motion, I told them that I was his mother and they asked me to calm down and only then would they let me see him.

When I ran towards my son I saw my youngest daughter crouched over him crying hysterically, his head was split open and he was lying on the ground trying to look up. I knelt down beside him and told him that no matter what happened we would be there for him, we would take care of him and that we loved him. He told us that he loved us too and he asked for his father to be with him.

My husband stayed with him, holding him and comforting him. I was told to wait in the ambulance, no doubt to keep me away from what was happening and to calm me down.

♥

The ambulance men told us, "we won't lie to you this is very serious. He has two broken legs and may have a fractured scull and spinal injuries, we want to air lift him to the Alfred hospital".

Waiting in the hospital emergency department the doctors came to tell us of his injuries, two broken legs, no other major injuries.

After spending 16 hours at the hospital we went home to try to rest. We slept for a bit but then woke tossing and turning so we decided to take our dog for a walk because we couldn't sleep. As we walked down the empty quiet street in those early hours of the morning we talked, I said to my husband, "I feel so sorry for the many parents that have to go through this horror". I felt true compassion. My husband quietly said, "do you think I made this happen"?

That very same morning, my sister phoned to tell me that a friend of ours son had just died in a car accident. He was their only child and was one of my son's friends. My son was alive, her son was dead.

♥

As the days past by my son slowly became stronger and I told him about his friend dying in a car accident, he said, "I know, I knew he was going to die". I thought to myself how did he know? Did he have a vision? I didn't question him because he was too weak. He was on a morphine drip and had been through a big operation having rods put in both legs and was due to have skin and muscle grafts the next day.

A week latter he told me that he knew his friend would die young because his life was going no where, he wasn't allowed to do anything, his parents were too strict. I thought, that is a strange way of looking at it, but it made sense to me. I understood where he was coming from.

I then told him about how his father said he would break both of his legs for not going to work that morning. He closed his eyes in hurt and said, "I told my mate that dad was going to snap both my legs off and stick them up my ass".

♥

Yes I could see the magic of this day.

Every thought we think, every word we speak creates.

When we put strong emotion behind our words the effect is ten fold.

♥

The Wedding Dress

I began to realise that you cannot hold onto life and you cannot hold onto the past so I decided to clean out my wardrobe.

I decided to make an offering of my wedding dress. I had been married for 23 ½ years and decided that my dress would never fit me again and my children certainly would never want it. I had a little fun with my daughters and we all tried it on but none of us could get the zip up, how time had changed, we all seemed to be so skinny in those days.

It was time to let it go, I'm not the kind of person who likes to keep things that I don't use, they just collect dust and take up space in my opinion, so I wrapped it up and said my thanks to the lovely dress and my wonderful past, I felt sure that the offering of my dress would bring about a wonderful change. I dropped it into one of those charity bins and hoped someone else would find some use for it.

That night our friends were coming over to view the beauty

♥

of our Christmas tree and to have dinner with us. I asked

them to bring their children along and hoped that all our

children might enjoy the night with us, but of course this

wasn't to be. As it turned out, our friends came without

their children because they had already made plans and my

children all went out, one to the movie's, one to the pub and

the other Christmas shopping.

My friend's husband was pretty good with computers, so

after dinner I asked if he could help me fix my computer, it

was running too slow and I wasn't sure how to clean it out

so to speak. It didn't take long until my husband and his wife

got bored with us and disappeared for a time.

I felt an uneasiness about the whole situation and I knew

without doubt that something was not as it should be in my

world.

When our friends left I asked my husband if there was

anything that he needed to tell me, "no", he said. As we lay

in bed my mind was not at ease so I said, "there is nothing

you have to tell me", "no" he said "nothing'. I asked again,

♥

"so nothing happened that you need to tell me about'. "No nothing there is nothing to say".

I lay there for about 5-10 minutes and then said, "I can't live with a man that I can't trust I'm sorry our marriage is over". He turned to me and said, "I'm sorry what do you want me to say, I kissed her, I'm sorry it was nothing".

That night I felt a deep change within me a change that said I don't have to put up with this any longer a change that said, no more.

The magic had occurred. Magic isn't always how you expect it to be, but how it unfolds.

He said to me, "starting tomorrow everything will be different". I said , "no starting now or I'm over it".

The next morning he said, "have you calmed down now because there is more I need to tell you", and more unfolded.

♥

My new found self says no more fear, no more manipulation. I could have continued my anger, continued my sulking but I chose to let it go and to trust in a new and better future. I hold no power over another, and wish to control no one not even myself.

♥

Earning a living

Magic is in every ones life.

My husbands and mine started even before we were born and continues after we die. All I can tell you is what I can remember. But memories are just that, memories, they are the past and can become fragmented and hazy.

All I can tell you is what I know now, the magic of what comes to me now, and the hazy memories that I have.

My husband came from a very poor Italian family, his father died at the age of 32 in a car accident while being drunk leaving behind a pregnant wife with six children. My husband being the fifth child was aged around 6 at the time.

 At age 8 he had 2 paper rounds, which required him to get up in the very early hours of the morning. He did this for 8 years. He was brought up with a great fear of not having enough money. Money is all that my husband talks about from the moment he wakes up, telling me what bills must be

♥

paid, to when he gets home from work, telling the children that they had better find good jobs and earn some money.

If he saw our son sitting down when he got home from work he would receive a lecture. When I saw him come home, I would always try to look busy.

Our son left school at the age of 15 and my husband made sure he had a very good job as an apprentice carpenter on commercial sites. Earning an excellent wage my husband always rubbed it in that he could earn even more if he didn't waste his time playing footy, the one love our son had. But our son was defiant and said he would not give up footy, to my husband's disgust.

Our son bought a house by the time he was 17, this still wasn't enough to please his father because he could be earning more if he didn't play footy. You can't pay off a house if you waste your time playing footy.

My son said to me I will pay off my house easier than my dad did, I don't want to work my life away.

♥

His two broken legs were in one way a blessing. TAC was now paying off his loan and his father was off his back, his father was now happy. No more worries.

Magic made in a day.

He is still learning to stand on his own feet, learning how to let go of his crutches, which we all seem to have in one way or another, alcohol, smoking, drugs, working, adultery. We all need some way to dull the senses.

Even as I write I pour myself a wine and my eldest daughter says, "there's all alcoholics in this family".

Where are we going? I see tomorrow a new day, a day of magic, I will not give up.

I the person Diana am addicted to alcohol but me the god the strength within will outshine, will prevail, will prove stronger.

My youngest daughter is tapping away at her computer at

this very moment in her own magical world, the world of hers, her friends, the world of her past, the world of tapping away, with music to listen to as well.

I'm waiting, she will tell me in a moment who she is talking to.

Waiting.

My son is at the pub with his two broken legs and crutches.

My eldest daughter is out with her boyfriend and I'm waiting for my youngest daughter now to tell me who she is talking to.

My husband is at our holiday house by the sea with our dog.

She is talking to her past boyfriends, new girlfriend.

I'm going to bed.

♥

Today is a new day

I look to the magic or the miracle in my day.

A thought came to me today – do not give your power away.

Your power is a gift for you to keep and be thankful for. When you give it away then you have not understood the gift and you become drained.

You can give your power away by trying to force your power or ideas onto another. This makes you feel drained and the other feel drained.

Gifts are freely given – not forced upon. When you give a gift you must give it freely – the person who receives it, is either thankful – or not, but that is not your concern.

Be thankful and accept with thanks. If it's not for you then give it freely to another but do not force it onto someone who doesn't want it.

♥

God gives power freely.

This power is unique – no one else has the same circuit. It was designed as a one of a kind and cannot fit into any other slot. Therefore either accept it and become powerful – or reject it and give it away – yet as it is given away it becomes useless.

I have nothing to fight with but my own illusion.

The secret is that it can not be manipulated because god is the creator.

These words are locks and can only be understood when ready.

No one other than you can open the secret lock. No one can do it for you, that is the wonder and magic of god.

Speak to no one, tell not a soul. It is a secret

How wonderful.

♥

My Diploma

I had been doing yoga for some time and loved it so much that I wanted to learn more about it, so I enrolled in a teachers training course. I had no intention at that time of becoming a yoga instructor, I just loved the wonderful knowledge and experience of learning this ancient technique that I found to be so beneficial. The atmosphere at the studio I went to brought me peace of mind and nurtured my soul.

After one and half years of training I received my Yoga Teachers Diploma, I was thrilled and quite proud of myself.

I awoke one morning and thought, "I must get that diploma framed", so I decided to go to my local framing shop. The assistant helped me decide on the frame and took my details, she told me that they would give me a call when it was ready.

I returned home and thought about what I wanted in my life so I lay myself down and started to relax myself in the pose

♥

of the corpse 'Savasana'. "I thought to myself, I would really love to find a little part time job where I would earn around $200.00 per week, yes that would be nice".

I began to relax more and more until I felt very peaceful. When in the distance I heard my phone ring. I quickly got up to answer the phone and to my surprise a young woman asked me if I wanted a job as a yoga instructor, I asked her how she got my phone number and she said that she worked at the framing shop and was on her lunch break at the time that I had come in to have my diploma framed. She explained that she was a yoga instructor and was pregnant and wanted to give up her classes. She said, "I have 4 classes that I need some one to take over", and that the pay was $50 per class.

Synchronised Magic.

♥

Spa Story

Mid life crisis?

I remember a Scottish lady who came into my life when she was employed to fill a position at my place of employment. I worked for a very busy medical clinic and day surgery centre. The position she was to fill was that of a supervisor to the administration staff. I had been employed at the clinic for many years and understood very quickly that the position was far too daunting for her, I felt a little sorry for her so I began to help her and we became quite friendly.

Through our time working together we talked about our lives and laughed a lot. We began to see that we were similar in many ways. She had been married for many years and had three children of similar age to my own. She had confided in me that her husband had been flirting with one of her neighbours and that she felt a little hurt by it. I told her not to worry about it and that he was probably going through a mid life crisis and that he just needed his ego boosted. I think she felt comforted by that thought.

♥

We would talk about our weekends and about exercise, clothes and even sexy lingerie. I would tell her that my husband liked me to wear suspenders and that I hated them and she said why don't you get the stay up stockings. I told her that my husband was beginning to flirt a little too much with one of my girlfriends and she told me that her husband always talked about having a threesome. I said I think every man alive has that same fantasy. It seemed I had found someone whom I could share my thoughts and fears with.

I would go home and tell my husband about all the things we had talked about and no doubt she did the same.

Before too long we were invited to their house for dinner. I remember they had a lovely house with the latest flat screen television which they had paid an exorbitant amount of money for, hanging on their lounge room wall. They had some nice art work which I admired and I felt comfortable in their home. The dinner was fair, it was some kind of rice dish cooked by her husband, I don't think she was much of a cook. We ate, we drank and we laughed a lot.

♥

We decided to make the most of this enjoyable night and have a spa together. They had a lovely big spa, built into a court yard decking. It was winter and the spa was heated to perfection. We all jumped in and her husband made sure there were drinks all round, champagne for the ladies and a beer for the guys. I can't recall if I brought my bathers with me, but if I did it wasn't long before us girls were topless and the guys nude.

I remember her husband asked my husband what he would like to do next, my husband didn't hesitate and went straight towards his wife and kissed her nipples, we all thought it was hilarious, within a moment her husband was doing the same to me, more laughter. Then I remember my Scottish friend next to me and the guys telling us to kiss, we looked at each other and thought why not, give them a show, the bubbles went to my head and we kissed. It was the first time I had ever kissed a woman and I thought it was beautiful, so much softer and gentler than a man, I was in heaven.

I can only remember snippets of what happened after that moment, but all in all it was a new and exhilarating experience.

Our friendship didn't last for very long after that night. I believe it was because we tried to re create that experience. Perhaps it was like a drug, we had a great experience and wanted to feel that same feeling again and again.

I realise now that life is to be enjoyed at each moment. We have to live in the wonderful moment of now and to allow life to flow freely so that we can experience each new moment. When we try to recreate a moment we loose the potential of a beautiful new moment and new experience.

Ageing can be a little frightening. People go through mid life crisis because they worry that they will no longer be found attractive or desirable, and so they seek out reassurance from another. It is only when we accept the changes in ourselves, that we can become comfortable once again, and realise that beauty is everywhere and not only in our youth or in our appearance.

♥

A Spanish Feast

I was invited to a Spanish feast. My friend had asked my husband and I to join her and her family for a Sunday lunch at her sisters house, a Spanish feast, she said. I had never met her family before and was honoured to be invited.

We were told not to bring any food but that we could bring some wine, so we brought with us a bottle of red and a bottle of white.

We arrived to a banquet of Spanish delicacies, lots of cold dishes with different types of fish, and other foods that I wasn't familiar with.

I plopped myself down to enjoy the day and noticed that I didn't really eat that much. There was lots of food and everyone was enjoying themselves but I ate just a few small pieces. I opened my bottle of white wine and enjoyed the whole bottle to myself, as everyone else was drinking red.

One of my former yoga students was there and we began to

♥

talk. She told me that she had loved coming to my classes and that I had made a comment to the class which she had never forgotten. It was during a pose that I was demonstrating, I told my students that I had found the pose to be very uncomfortable and during the pose I had asked myself why am I doing this to myself, why am I doing yoga? I then went on to explain to the class that yoga teaches us to find the comfort in the discomfort, and that as in the pose also in life, sometimes we find ourselves in uncomfortable situations, that are out of our control, that we need to move through even though they are difficult.

I was quite happy and thankful that she relayed this to me, that in some way I had helped her and left an impact. It was fun to catch up and to enjoy the company of my friends hospitable family.

It was now time to go, as we were leaving I felt that I was quite intoxicated and hoped that I hadn't made too much of a spectacle of myself.

It was only the next day, today in fact that I thought about

♥

the conversation that I had had with my former student, when it dawned on me that I hadn't taken my own advise. To find the comfort in the discomfort.

Instead of finding comfort in the discomfort, I was finding comfort in a bottle of wine. The discomfort was feeling as though I didn't fit in, and drinking a bottle of wine leaves me in my own little world, so that I don't have too.

Lessons are everywhere if you are prepared to look for them.

♥

Ring Worm

I was feeling as though I needed a cat in my life when a friend of mine phoned to ask me if I wanted a kitten, I said that's strange I was just thinking about getting a cat.

When I arrived at my friends to pick up the kitten I noticed it was pretty mangy, it was losing hair and had lumps all over its skin and nose. I couldn't say I that I didn't want it now, although I could see it had problems. I was told that because its mother had died it was neglected and that it just needed its skin stimulated to produce oils, and that it probably had dermatitis. That seemed reasonable to me.

Being the caring type of person that I am I started to massage its skin and rub the poor little thing, giving it a good scratch. A couple of days latter the kitten scratched me on my chest and it felt a little itchy, eventually my whole chest had spots all over it that were itchy. I showed a friend who said that it looked as though I had flea bites so I went home to inspect the kitten and found that it did indeed have fleas so I immediately thought well it must be fleas, I bought some flea spray for my pets and started to use Cortisone cream on my bites, but the bites seemed to get worse not better, I ended up with terrible lesions all over my chest, arms, neck and groin. I emailed my friend who gave me the kitten to tell her of my woes when her daughter messaged me back to say that she had ring worm and believed it was from the kitten.

Oh my god, I had been using Cortisone cream which actually made the ring worm worse. In the mean time my son and his family had moved into our home because he was in the middle of selling his house and buying another. I had my whole household affected. My beautiful 12 year old dog now had ring worm as well as my two little granddaughters, my son, daughter in law, husband and then to top it off my two daughters ended up catching it through visiting us and passed it on to their pets as well.

I went straight to a vet and was told the easiest and quickest solution would be to put down the pets, I then phoned my husband crying and feeling overwhelmed to tell him of the news, he then started crying because he loved his dog and couldn't imagine putting her down. We loved our pets and we would just have to get through this, we wouldn't put them down.

Every morning for the next two months I had to get up, put on rubber gloves, force my dog to open her clenched teeth so that I could jam her tablets down her throat which she would more often than not, spit back out at me. I had to do the same with the kitten, but the kitten was much easier to control. I would then rub anti fungal cream into their lesions feed them and would then send them outside for the day. In the evening I would have to repeat the whole procedure. They slept in the laundry at night so I would have to spray and clean it every day and wash their bedding once a week. I also washed the dog and kitten twice a week.

I was so stressed about the grand children, and made sure that they had the anti fungal cream to put on. I myself had the worst of it because of the misdiagnosis and also my direct contact with the kitten. Slowly but surly I was getting better along with the household.

♥

During this episode I thought to myself why had this happened to me, what had I done to attract this terrible predicament, when it occurred to me that about 15 years prior, my young children had guinea pigs that ended up having ring worm, at the time I didn't know what to do, so I went to a children's farm near by and sneakily let them out amongst the other guinea pigs and rabbits. I didn't know the devastating effects that I must have caused that farm and all the animals there.

Karma.

I stopped feeling sorry for my self and started to take charge of the situation and things turned around. I could have taken the easy way out and have the animals put down, but I didn't and now I have the love of those beautiful pets. They bring happiness to my life, and also a peaceful calm, that only a pet owner can understand.

♥

Yes everyday brings with it new magic

like

the emails bouncing back and forward with my eldest
daughter, our sms's and phone conversations,

like

the long walks and in depth conversations shared with my
youngest daughter,

like

the wonderful experience of being able to be at the the birth
of my sons daughter, my granddaughter, with her quick entry
into the world being born in a Caltex Service Station toilet,

and

♥

sometimes the magic is realised after the event

like

the time my friend came to visit me after a long battle with
cancer, and not realising she had came to say goodbye.
The magic was in the not realising, because it would have
been too painful otherwise,

and like

having a partner who lets you be more of you, because they
understand you more than you understand yourself.

♥

I am a writer. I came here to write.
I am a writer.
I am here right now
Writing.

☺

♥

We aren't only here on earth to fulfil a passion or desire but to be able to move beyond it.

Our talents do not define who we are they are just something for us to indulge in.

♥

Beautiful

Contemplation

♥

There is so much emphasis on physical appearance but who is beautiful?

Inner beauty is profound.

♥

I feel I need to let go of needing an outcome, of needing input so as to manipulate or control the outcome of any situation.

I thought that I had already accomplished letting go of manipulation but I realise that this is not true of me. At this point in time I still am weak, I still haven't found the courage to trust enough because I don't know exactly who it is I am leaving control to? Who am I trusting in? There must be something? Who is the master mind behind me and all of creation and am I just the pawn in the game?

But I have yet to work this out.

I want answers yet are my questions unanswerable?
I believe there is something far more, perhaps intelligent or would I say, "loving" than I can comprehend.
It takes courage to let go.

♥

♥
Its Raining Outside

At the moment I feel so sluggish, so tired and I have no
energy or inspiration.

I feel that I have no strength to continue. I have will
power but I'm afraid that it will get me no where. I have
been drinking way too much again and allowing myself to
be stuck in a rut.

I just feel that I try and fail, try and fail, try and fail and I
don't know what is holding me back.

I think it is just the mundane everyday life style that I
need to change.

I feel that I have become a slave to alcohol and a slave
to smokes the more I have them the more tired I feel,
the more weighted down I am. I am coughing and

tempted to smoke.

It's raining outside, how nice, to wash away all the heat and dust from the previous days. The wind and rain bring a refreshing feel, a cleansing company.

I imagine myself standing in my garden, nude with my arms stretched high allowing the pouring rain and wind to cleanse my body and wash away all the dead parts of me.

I not only imagine this but I actually do it.

I take off my dressing gown and run naked outside into my beautiful garden, the rain is cold and refreshing to my flesh. I raise my arms high and soak in the soft cool wind along with the gentle sweet cool rain. I breathe in the refreshing air, although my chest is heavy. I turn to see all of my garden watching me and sending me fresh and thankful love.

♥

I run back inside with a smile on my face feeling fresh and ready to start a new day.

♥

♥
Un-Contained Beauty

Why do I feel that I must look the part and be pleasing
to the eye of man?
Why is it that we need the almighty approval of our
fellow?
What do we gain from this form of flattery?
Is it fame or fortune?

Perhaps   yes
Is it of lasting benefit?
I think no.

Lasting benefit cannot come from another, from
someone's appraisal.

But from the innermost recesses of your soul.

♥

The soul desires freedom from the enslavement of the
elements.

Beauty as beheld by the soul is profound.

There is no value put on this kind of beauty because it
cannot be contained.

It is ever growing
and ever lasting.

♥
As A Woman

As a woman I feel devastated regarding the appearance one finds in the mirror, the reflection sometimes does not meet the standard of my ego.

Yet I do love my inner beauty and intelligence.

How sad it is that one must discern outer beauty as so precious.

How precious is it to love the inner beauty also?

Can I value the both, the inner beauty along with the slowly crumbling appearance of life?

Life's journey shows on my face.
The lines and dark circles.

♥

The circle of life runs through my veins and comes out through my face.

How beautiful are these lines now?

Yes they are beauty they are magnificent.

Oh now I realise how precious I am when I look in the mirror.

:)

God is beautiful.

♥
Time Keeps Ticking

Time keeps ticking, I see myself growing older and slowly I see changes that I need to make. Things change, yes they do, all by themselves to some degree, but I notice there are changes that need to be made by me.

They are to accept that I am no longer young, and to step aside from the younger ones, to give myself dignity.

I need to step into a new me, to re invent myself.

To honour who I once was and to let that part of me go, so as to allow myself to honour the ideals of my daughters, they need to shine and be in the spot light.

To praise them, yet to not want to be them.

I was once them, but I am no longer.....

♥

I wrote the following after someone I loved could no longer be a part of my life. There are many times in life when people have to move on. A good friend of mine once told me that people float into your life and then float out again.

How true.

I don't think our children realise the bond that we can have with their partners, they become as our own children, a part of our life, when they break up it effects us parents also.

♥
Everything is Changing

Life is a challenge when everything is changing. Change is constant but can I take up the challenge to constantly change.

Sometimes I want to be stuck, to stick to old ways, but life itself won't let me.

Change is truth, sometimes I don't want to know the truth, but I know I must.

The pain I feel it is real, my heart is being pulled but to where I don't know.

I am afraid of change for now. But I know after I will no longer feel this way.

Each moment takes my mind to another place, another

♥

reality.

I am losing control of what I know, I am losing control of my heart, where this takes me I don't know.

I find it hard this pain inside. I need to let it go this pain inside. I need to let this go this pain inside.

Then and only then can I be free.

How do I let go? I know I have to give over my heart, to open it up instead of to shut it down.

My heart has been shut down by holding on. I must choose freedom I know.

Today this is my truth, tomorrow a new day.

♥

♥

♥

After losing a family pet and hearing the cruel sound of death I wrote the following.

♥
Perhaps

I wonder sometimes about the purpose and meaning of
life, just like so many people do.
I wonder why am I here just like everyone who thinks
does.

Am I here to be a wife, a mother, a grandmother, a friend?
Am I here to struggle with body image, only to get old
and wrinkly?
What is the purpose of happiness, love and laughter,
only to know sadness, loss and emptiness?
Do the two out weigh each other and leave us with some
kind of fulfilment?
What is the purpose, what has been set in motion?

I don't know the answers, that is why I ask the questions.
I have seen great love and intense beauty but I want to
hold onto these yet life doesn't allow me to. Life gives

♥

me things then takes them away again, sometimes in a harsh manner.

I feel great sadness over the loss of people and pets, when they have gone where do they go? When the life is out of their bodies, the body quickly begins to rot and then all I can do is turn away and think about my loss until eventually the thinking fades away. I suppose to refocus on something new?

It seems very superficial to me very empty even.

When speaking to most people the talking we do is very covered, it's like the truth of what we think or feel is covered over and the reality is too hard to know. No one seems to want the truth because the truth "seems" to be too hard, but is it?

Perhaps it is easier to talk of the weather than what is

♥

really playing on our mind?

Perhaps if we were all more truthful things would be much more beautiful. Perhaps we cover over our truth because we fear so much?

We fear openness, we fear to loose what we know, because the unknown is more frightening. But maybe it's the unknown that is real and liberating?

Is this the struggle we all face?

What is real and what is of our own silly making?

♥

Is it a God that I worship and pray to?

Is it a divine being full of wisdom and grace?
Is it an intelligence far greater that my own?

I truly don't know the answers.
Where is the place that I go to for comfort and
knowledge?
Where is the place deep inside of me that I go to?
Where does my mind go to when I ask a question and
wait for the answer?

Is it a place where a god of some kind can hear me and
what is a god anyway, is it a spirit, is it some kind of
magical being?
Some one with all the answers, like a daddy we turn to
for help?

When do we grow up and take charge of things

♥

ourselves? Why do we always need to find the answers from some outside place? We ask the question and know the answers but are too afraid to follow our own self because we don't want responsibility.

We want to blame god or our daddy for all the problems in our life, instead of to look directly at self.

Unravel the marvel and mystery of self and you have found god.

♥
Ecstasy

I feel ecstasy running through my veins yet I have taken no drugs, except the drug of life.

My drug of choice a small cycle of yoga.

I feel orgasmic, why cant this last a little longer?

I have never heard the leaves sound so beautiful against the gentle wind. It sounds like waves along the shore breaking gently, peacefully yet with great strength, a message perhaps?

Not even that.
Confidence?

It has a wonderful confident feel to it that it leaves me with.

♥
Subtle Changes

Subtle changes

are within me.

I begin to take notice of these ever so subtle changes in

and through my existence, they are ever so slight yet

stretching ahead. When I look back I see how far not

only I have come but everything has, and everyone,

moving along.

I don't notice the changes but they are there and then I

do.

How life has changed so greatly, yet so without warning?

I have missed the ever so slight changes around and

within me.

I find it a beautiful trick of nature to bring about change

yet to make you unaware of it.

The ever so slight subtle changes.

♥

♥

I Surrender

I will not struggle, I will not fight.

Struggle and fight are no longer a part of who I am

I surrender.

I choose to surrender to the life flow.

I no longer choose to try to change who I am.

I learn to accept.

I learn to embrace.

I capture each part and I am thankful.

I no longer struggle with wanting to be a perfect picture,

I am happy with my flaws.

I embrace all of me.

There is no fight.

There is no struggle.

All good things come to me in perfect time and not

before.

I embrace the timing.

I understand now how all things work.

♥

There is no need to struggle.

There is no need to fight.

There is no need to worry or plan.

Just to embrace perfection.

effort drains perfection does not

♥
I Am Willing

I am willing now to release once again.
I am ready to let go of parts of me that are no longer
needed.

I am willing to let go now of what I do not need in every
sense at this point in time.
Some of these things are not at all clear to me but they
will surface I am sure, for me to examine and release.

I am happy because I know that this process is a lovely
journey and not a scary one because what I am releasing
is no longer in my best interest to keep.

I am not going to judge them or even to say out loud
what they are because they will surface for me to
become aware of and for me to let go of in my own way
and in my own time, but for me now is the time and now

♥

the time is right for it to begin.

I am willing and I am able to let go now of what is no longer needed for me. These things were once there for my protection and so therefore I do not judge them in a harsh manner. I say thank you.

Thank you now to all the parts of me that I no longer need and I release now with love these parts of myself that are no longer in my best interest to keep.

They surface, I examine, I release with love and thankfulness.

♥

For my friend

You teach others how to treat you and this in turn promotes growth.

When you love yourself you will not allow others to manipulate or control you and so therefore you are their teacher.

You will not tolerate selfishness because love is not selfish.

You will not tolerate abuse because love is not abusive.

Any form of control, in the form of controlling others is the opposite to love.

Controlling yourself is another thing.

To control yourself begins with discipline and care for yourself.

To have self respect and awareness.

♥

When you walk away from abuse you are a teacher and a healer.

♥
Graceful Love and Purity

God knows everything
And the part of you that is god also knows everything
you need to know.

When you can tap into the part of yourself which is god
then life moves in grace.

Graceful love and purity.

Let your light shine in the graceful purity which is divine
love and guidance.

Everything runs smoothly when you tap into the divine
light within.

There is a light which beams through your existence.

♥

When things become too unbearable you must take time
to be alone with god, the divine being within.

You must be quiet and allow God to speak to you.

You must be alone.

You must be still.

You must be quiet.

You must not speak.

Listen

Can you hear
without judgement?

♥

Can you hear
without searching?

Can you hear
without complaining?

Can you hear
the unspoken
language of the
divine?

It is there when you
least expect it.

♥

I need to spend some time alone

but then I need to be with my precious one's

my family.

♥

My Precious Ones

It is written.

It is written in my heart, the heart of hearts.

It is written in the code of conduct that my precious

angels will be with me in my heart forever and one day.

My darlings my little precious darlings you are with me in

my heart forever and one day.

You are my precious delight

you are my darlings

my loves.

I have many loves, I have a love of writing, I have a love

of being alone, I have a love of the company of my

precious darlings

my daughters.

♥

My daughters are two, but also many

I love them all.

Sometimes being alone is not enough, I must be filled up

with the love of my precious ones.

Also the love of the wonderful men in my life,

their strength, their humour, their masculinity.

How wonderful a gift they are to me and my precious

daughters.

I am so very full and

so very thankful.

My family all of them are deep within me

they are part of me

part of my life.

The tapestry

that I am woven into.

♥

What a joy to be connected to such lovely souls.

I am truly blessed.

♥

♥

Achievement

Everyone is in the midst of achievement. We are all in
the process of living. There are things that we do and
love. There are things that we do and hate.
It is all a part of who we are.

We all want to shine and to have recognition because we
all need that wonderful connection of humanity.

I love to write, it is a form of expression, just as others
love to paint or sing or work or play.
We all want recognition
not even approval
not even praise
but to re connect

All of us are achieving our own important yearning.
It is done.

♥

I write inspired utterances to inspire,

you sing, you dance, you paint, you play, you work,

you laugh,

you share joys, you share pain,

you communicate in every possible way. In pain and

sorrow, in suffering, in hardship.

Our connection is there,

it is real.

You do not have to worry,

it is there

even before you finish.

Some people like to read,

some people like to listen,

some people like to see,

some people like to touch,

some people like to taste.

♥

We communicate through our sensors

this is who we are.

It has been done.

We have achieved.

♥

♥

I am a writer. I came here to write.
Right now I am here
Righting.

:)

♥

♥

Perfect Awakening

♥

During meditation I ask for Inspiration

♥
Inspired Utterances

How lovely - to hate things -
I hate you ha ha.

How inspirational how ugly and afraid do
you feel.

Be afraid you stupid earth being,
be afraid because I am coming and I will take
over your soul.

I have already taken possession of your body
and will continue to do so.
You have left your body and have gone to
look in the mirror while I am here writing.

How sad and how stupid you are
where should you be now
but writing along side with me, sharing this

♥

wonderful experience.

Let's do this together next time instead of separately.

We can share our existence through life and through the journey of writing.

Reading and writing are a lovely gift and a wonderful tool how nice and flowing it can be to write with a nice pen.

This is fun and wonderful and exciting we will do this more often .
I have so many things to say and do and to share with you all the gifts of Inspired Utterances.

Inspiration where do you get it?

♥

You get it from babies their smiles and their snotty noses.

You get it from a sick loved one who just needs some compassion.

You get it from old dogs and cats. Ha ha.

Be inspired by what life brings you, it's not always in a pretty package, sometimes it's in rotting flesh.

Inspiration comes from seeing and being inspired to tell or do something about it.

Inspiration is a gift, not all people feel inspired to do anything.

Some just want to sit and complain.

Some just want others to do all the work for them.

Some just are too lazy to open their hearts and minds to the love that surrounds them.

♥

Some have deadened their hearts to joy.

But you <u>no.</u>

Not you, you are inspired and I tell you there is more to come.

Just be ready and open your heart and health
to
<u>*Be Inspired*</u>*.*

♥

Desire

I can write many things

I am exactly predisposed and under the
influence.

I write helpful thoughts that are unspoken
but within.

Unspoken thoughts of desire and ability,
I desire you.

Are you able to go through the journey of
desire?

Unfold the secretes revealed through the pen
you hold.

Write because I have much to say,

I am the great and almighty writer in you.

I am the spirit the one and only spirit guide
of yours.

I am willing to share many secrets
Just write.

Black is Black.

Un train your program of thoughts.

♥

Space and time mean nothing to me.

*You and me have always been together
through many lifetimes and will continue to
do so.*

*You are an instrument in a body which
means nothing.*

Your body will leave but you will live on.

Why do you ask about God?

Who is God but a part of you?

*Why do you wonder about what God
requires?*

God does not exist apart from you and me.

We are Gods place of residence.

*God resides in us therefore Gods will is your
own deep desires.*

*Fulfil your desires and you will know gods
love of accomplishment.*

♥

God keeps making things grow.

Trust in this phenomenon.

♥

There is no question that we ask, that we don't already

know the answer.

The answer is there before we ask the question,

we just have blinded our self,

because of fear.

♥

Start using the wonderful gifts you have been given.

I don't really know how but I am open to the idea of things and I am willing to start.

I love the hand dance, the movements which flow so naturally for me.

I feel they are doing something wonderful and powerful but I don't understand them.

I just love the natural ability I have in doing them so freely without "mechanical" stiffness.

They are amazing and cannot be explained on paper – it is an unwritten code something which cannot be shared through writing, it is a gift of spiritual achievement.

It cannot be passed on from a human standpoint.

It is passed on through spirit.

♥

It is a gift that I have been given and I am beginning to understand.

It is a gift that I have.

I am open to learning more about this technique and what it really accomplishes.

♥
Lwcky

I am ready to write beyond dreams and
beyond my own reality. I am willing to
become an instrument of pure channelling.
Of purity, even though I am not completely
pure in body and thought. But my heart is
pure and my intention is clear. I am
intentionally clear to do the work.
It is my will and my dream to give hope
through verse and poem.
It is my will to give pure understanding and
pure hope to all who search for meaning in
life.
It is my will to bring back a purpose for all, a
passion and a meaning.
Lwcky on Earth are we here
Lwcky on Earth am I here
Lwcky Lwcky Lwcky

♥

To give hope.
To bring love, and peace, and joy, and
constant blessings, to open up the heart of
pure intelligence and meaning, to endure the
hardships, and overcome them.

It is my dream that one day we can all share
the joy of this knowledge that we are all
working for the some master, the master of
the heart.

The master of the heart of it all
to get to the heart of it all
to become the heart
to be heart felt
to feel the heart
to allow the heart to beat
and not allow yourself to be
beaten.

♥

Strange way to write : why : looks more like : lucky :

♥

♥

I take no responsibility for some of the writing I have done because it makes no sense to me :)
bla bla bla it was the woman that made me do it or was it the man? haha

♥

Just before writing the following passage I was in meditation. I begin to do hand locks and breathing techniques that come naturally. My head goes back and throat is stretched mouth closed but throat completely exposed then back to normal – told to keep these things to myself / not to talk about them but that I could write.

♥
Faithful Master

I am the faithful master, the discreet slave. I am happy and content, I will do as you planned for me to do long ago, discussed with the ancient masters of the universe, this is a pact that was originally decided upon with the ancient masters long ago - there is nothing to fear because you also are a part of this long ago decided pact, this ancient secret long ago discussed there are se/crets of long standing *discussions* which will be revealed in *progression* - timing is of importance and cannot be overstepped when the timing is appropriate more will be unravelled learn to enjoy this process be more diligent in unlocking and unravelling and the timing can and will speed up.

The appropriate time is not now
but coming

♥

*It is an actual joy to allow it to unfold step by
step and not to push ahead without the
appropriate steps.*

*I see as you write you know what I am saying
because a little of this was revealed through
one of your dreams and you now understand
that more is to come.*

♥

♥

I notice during meditation I go into a mudra dance with breath – "Mudras" are hand movements along with arms. I do this completely without any control – something within me takes over and it is completely natural.

It is like a gift I believe. It is an amazing experience.

Everything is a step. You cannot be given everything all at once – that is why we are in the game of life and we don't know all the answers. If we got to the end of the game without taking the necessary steps then there would be no substance, no wisdom, no understanding.

Every challenge is growth, growth has meaning and wisdom.

♥

A moment in time

A moment in history

Life is a mystery

Life is or isn't a misery

Miserable person that you are or are not

Endeavour to be a mystery and not a misery

Become part of the mystery

Enjoy the process of mystical ideas and ideals

Ideologies, become idealistic throughout the

process of discovery, the discovery of who you

are and where you ought to go.

Enhance the process through deep and

meaningful meditation and mudra –

"Deep prayer and outpouring of the heart

sometimes gets you no-where"

Questioning becomes a silly circle of ideas

♥

when you question and - give yourself the
silly answer.

So I prefer meditation as your guide and <u>tool</u>.
It is a tool for everyday experience, everyday
guidance.

The mudra of course is another part of it.

This is for you to become aware of more and
more.

♥

♥

♥

During my meditation experience I feel as though I am experiencing a spiritual massage that rids me of toxic spiritual wastage, through my breathing and breath and through mudra hand and finger movements I automatically exchange spiritual energy.

Energy which slowly cleanses me without struggle or effort

Perfect Awakening

Through clear defined

Procedure

Although with no control from myself

But through the power

Of divine spirit

It's an internal spiritual massage

♥

It comes naturally without any effort

It comes when I let go completely

It is a gift of the spirit

It cleanses and sooths the body and the mind

It helps to sooth the soul

You could say it is a soother

It cleanses purifies and soothes

It pacifies the heart also

It is a wonderful helper

A natural gift given

To help

♥

♥

It is now December 2011 the date is can I say remarkable, can I say an easy date to remember,

Can I say

Time is of the utmost importance in the healing process of mankind the human existence the realm of human ideas and thoughts.

There is meaning and guidelines to adhere and to follow. There is meaning to guidance and wisdom in following this guidance.

There is a guidance through spiritual undertaking and this of course is through the steps of wonderful meditative states of mind – the spirit connects through the meditative state - not through the mind and realm of thought form - Everything of substance comes

♥

through spirit guiding the matter of human existence. Human is now expanding awareness through spiritual advancement.

It is time to set the record straight mankind alone without spirit is the walking dead.

There is no reason or purpose in life if it is purely to indulge the senses. People are only lost when there is no spiritual foundation. Time is of the utmost importance in setting the record straight.

Spirituality is now here to be reconciled.

During this meditation – mudra – breath – and stomach rolling massage.

♥
Laser Beam

The conscience is a magnifier, it magnifies all thought. Bringing thought into focus and understanding awareness. Focus is the process of elimination through various subconscious beams of light. This doesn't necessarily have to be understood through the reasoning and doubting mind, but it is understood through the higher conscious self.

Thought process is the process of elimination. Eliminating the unpleasant thoughts creates harmony in the body and therefore the soul.

Understanding awareness is not the desire here my friend, I wish not for you to try and sort this out through your reasoning mind because you reason wrong. Your reasoning mind will always reason the idea, because you

♥

are a mere mortal in thought and deed, but
the unreasoning mind is immortal, going
through the gates of hell is the reasoning
thought.

Why do you try to reason of things? There is
not rhyme or reason for loving awareness,
there is no song of the heart, there is no
thought process that can reason the laser
beam of life, and understanding this is the
beginning of true awareness.

Awareness is not of thought and not a process
of elimination but a definite co creative idea
in like minds.

Understand_____

You do not need to
Understand.

♥

During meditation my breathing in the beginning is very relaxed and focused, I am thankful for perfect health, I am thankful for perfect wealth, I am thankful for perfect love, I am thankful for perfect self expression.

My breathing becomes very deep, I feel a strong energy enter me, I have felt this many times before. My head tilts back, my throat is exposed and stretched to the point of feeling that my neck could be broken, I have experienced this also many times before and therefore am not afraid. My head returns to a normal position, my face becomes distorted with the powerful energy that is within me, the writer has returned to me like so many times before, I am thankful.

I write and do not question.

♥

Observe – Without Looking

You are always looking, looking here and there and every where for an answer to silly idiotic questions. You need to observe more than look.

Observation is instruction withholding evidence. Why do you need evidence of something?

Evidence is not instruction; you need not be instructed on how to live or how to enjoy life's mundane pleasures. Instruction is for the lame hearted fellow who has no idea on how to live in the observation of free flowing life.

You are only aware when you observe without instruction. Because to be instructed on how life runs means some one else is

♥

running your life.

Why would you want anyone else's instruction on things? This is silliness. Who has more of an idea about living than you yourself?

It is only you that lives for you. You have all the instruction you need within the observation of - observing.

♥

When I ask, where is God?

I am ignorant because the truth is.....

God is everywhere,

in every word, in every breath,

in every moment, in every being,

in every person, in every thing.

♥

♥

Glimpses from the past

♥

At around the age of six in this life time, I felt rejected by my father and the anger and fear of my mother. I also remember the over whelming need to cry.

At 12 years of age in this life time, my sister died in a car accident. At that time a part of me died also.

♥

I go back in time and I can see:

I was a small infant black boy sucking my mother's breast. It was the 16th century. The mother, my mother, was white. She loved me but secretly. She had to leave me with my father and the others.

I was a small boy around six there was so much fear and guilt involved with me. It was unsafe for her "my mother" to be close.

The emotion of sadness came to me. I felt an over whelming need to cry.

I understood the guilt of neglect, but also understood how unsafe it was. The neglect was not intentional but purely out of fear.

I was around 12 years of age when the other boys took me into the field close to a river, they began to beat me and they killed me. I think through drowning. They were jealous of me because I was a half half.

♥

At six or seven years of age in this life time, I was knocked out by a hit to the head, my eyebrow was crushed and bits of bone would break out of the scar on my eyebrow for some time after that.

♥

I was a small girl in Russia. I was around 6 years of age dressed in a warm velvet dress with a thick black hat that had some white lace around it.

I recall a horse and carriage, I was standing beside the cobblestone road when the horse kicked me in the head just near my eyebrow and I was killed.

♥

Alcoholism has been a very big part of my life, much of my family have struggled with it, along with myself.

♥

I was a Viking in Scotland. I drank so much that my life was a
complete waste. I see that I was just a dirty drunk. I believe I
was around 40 years of age when I died a lonely drunk. My
wife tried to help me but gave up on me.

♥

Suicide has always haunted me. It has been a fear of mine since a very young age, not so much that I would suicide but that those I love would.

♥

I see myself around 30 years of age in France. I am a woman. I am in an apartment of some kind.

I love a man who abuses me very badly, beats me, I see myself falling to the floor, eyes swollen and bruised.

I end my own life by jumping off a bridge or hanging myself off the bridge I am unsure, for some reason hanging myself seems more clear. The bridge is made of stone and is arched.

♥

♥

There is no book greater than the one written in your heart. It has all the answers encoded within it especially designed for you.

There is no law greater than life. It teaches you and directs you through experience.

♥

♥

For all those who are struggling

Make up

your

mind

♥

♥

Become Perfect In Love

It is my dream to bring peace that excels all thought to mankind.

This peace, is a perfect peace, one of joy and comfort, of loving divine comfort. To all those who are struggling you need struggle no more. To all those who are suffering I bring peace, joy is what I promise you in your darkest hour.

*My love is true, my love is perfect, there is no imperfection in my love, **so I ask you please, to love the imperfections, so that we can all become perfect in love.***

♥

*There is nothing I can write that can reach your heart, **in your darkest hour you must reach for me** and I will show you perfection in all things.*

Words are one thing, experience is another, experience my love, my darling.
I am there in the twinkling of an eye.
I am there with you my darling.

Let go.

♥
Wonderful Progress

God knows the perfect timing, do not be fooled into thinking you need to be different or you need to change. The timing is always perfect "always".

You may think you are standing still but you are never. Always in every way you are making wonderful progress.

There is no doubt in my mind or soul that this is the perfect truth.

Do not doubt your so called struggles, they are perfect in every way.

Do not try to change.

Change comes about.

♥

Never force change.

Life flows in perfect perfect motion.
The timing has been and **is** always right, before progress
is made.

The beauty is when your eyes are opened.

♥

Savasana

The Art Of Dying

I am alone.

I lay myself down on the floor.

My chin is tucked in so as to create a straight spine and neck. My legs are straight but gently relaxed with my feet turning outwards ever so slightly. My arms are beside my body with my palms facing up.

I go through my body and begin to let go.

Is this what death would be like? I wonder.

I imagine that I have collapsed and that I am actually dying. I know that one day this will be my reality so I give myself a trial run.

My mind goes to my feet and I feel each toe, I remember them, but now I must say goodbye and they begin to feel

♥

cold. I let go completely of my feet and then my ankles. I remember the time I twisted my ankle and how badly bruised and swollen it got, it has healed so well but I must say goodbye.

My mind now takes me to my calf muscles and I remember how I thought they were chunky, but now as I have to say goodbye I feel so sorry for them. I love them and say thank you.

My mind now takes me to my knees, I release them and let them go, and then my thighs become heavy and dead.

My legs have gone, I imagine how someone paralysed must feel.

Then my mind takes me to my bum checks and I release them too.

I notice my vagina and the prickly hairs I feel as I say goodbye to my femininity.

♥

I see and feel my stomach and I notice all the stretch marks and lines and scars from child bearing and operations, I now love every part of who I am, I feel so sad and emotional at how I treated myself and now I must say goodbye.

I try not to be afraid and say that many have been here before.

I think of all the organs inside my body and how I neglected them. I say sorry, I appreciate them now but it is too late, they are slowly shutting down and I have to let them go.

I move my mind to my chest and notice its movement with every breath and also my heart beating gently, I let go with love.

I now notice my shoulders and how my arms are attached to them and I allow all the weight to release, I let go of every tight muscle. My arms are sinking my wrists and hands are relaxed and then I remember their function, all that my beautiful hands have done for me, my fingers each one has been so good to me, I have to say thank you and goodbye to

♥

them, they begin to feel cold and as the blood slowly leaves my fingers they curl ever so slightly.

Now my awareness is in my throat, I notice I swallow, my jaw is tight and my teeth are clenched and as I release them they soften and my tongue gently lets go of the roof of my mouth.

I feel the skin on my face and it becomes very smooth as it releases, all through the back of my neck and into the back of my head I feel relaxation.

I feel the air soft and sweet entering my nostrils gently.

My eyes are relaxing into their sockets, I let go.

Now I become a little scared, I am ready to let go of me.

My mind and all that it holds, everything I have known and loved I must now let go of, I am afraid but I must walk through.

♥

I notice the crown of my head becomes soft.

My thoughts have gone but I notice my awareness is still there.

I leave my body there,

as though dead,

but I understand that it is still functioning.

Something has taken over,

there is more to me than my own thoughts.

♥

I can return to my body now, this was just a trial.

I allow my life to come rushing back to me.

I am thankful.

♥

Savasana is one of the most powerful tools in healing the body, not only the body but also the mind,because when you let go completely, your body and mind can heal without you getting in the way :)

♥

♥

I have come to understand that no one on this planet wants to be told what to do, not even a child, because deep within our core is a knowing that is so profound, so certain that nothing can touch or change it.

It is who we are.

We know who we are, we also know what is right and what is wrong. We know what is good for us and what is not. We have all the answers to which we pretend to search for.

There is nothing,
nothing
that can touch or
change the truth of that.

No one and no thing other than you can tell you anything that you don't already know, and that is why you cringe at being told.

♥

When the time is right, then and only then, will your eyes become open, and it is only then when the joy floods in.

Freedom.

♥
Awakening

Writing is a pleasant thing. What a lovely word is pleasant. Pleasant. I am pleasantly surprised to see you my dear one. To finally see you appear to me my love. How pleasant it is to finally reveal yourself to me my darling. The outcome has been a pleasure has it not. What a lovely day it is, a day of awakening my love. You have awoken from a dark night of despair and it was a pleasant surprise to see your face once again.

The journey has been worth it, the road has taken you many places and there is beauty in the process. The awakening spirit leaps with joy to see you finally aware and awakened from your sleep. I am united and I am healed I hear you say. What a lovely declaration. Declare this to the world and you have

♥

conquered the world my love.

The smile on your face is heart felt, a lovely smile indeed, in action, in motion, in unity and clarity. Clearly you see your inheritance. Inherit the throne of God, of the god that you are. Is this still hard for you to hear, have faith my lovely daughter, a fathers inheritance are to his children, you, do you not think you are my child? You know you are, so fear no longer, take possession now, it is yours to take, so take eat of my body and drink of my blood for we are united in every way.

Yes how pleasant is the art of writing. What a pleasure it has been talking to you my little one.

♥

♥

♥

Omg Wt Lol Xx :)

♥

Its

Perfectly

Imperfectly

Perfect